Oh, Brother ...
Oh, Sister

A Sister's Guide to Getting Along

by Brooks Whitney Phillips

★American Girl®

illustrated by Laura Cornell

Published by American Girl Publishing

Copyright © 1999, 2008 by American Girl

Questions or comments? Call 1-800-845-0005, visit our Web site at **americangirl.com**, or write to Customer Service, American Girl, 8400 Fairway Place, Middleton, WI 53562-0497.

Printed in China

12 13 14 15 16 LEO 10 9 8 7 6 5

All American Girl marks are trademarks of American Girl.

Editorial Development: Andrea Weiss, Michelle Watkins

Art Direction: Kym Abrams

Design: Ingrid Hess, Camela Decaire

Production: Gretchen Krause, Mindy Rappe, Jeannette Bailey, Judith Lary

Illustrations: Laura Cornell

At our grandparents' house in Montana. That's me in the middle.

With Deed and Mandy on my 7th birthday. I'm the tall one.

Dear Reader,

I'll never forget the summer my little sister, Mandy, insisted on tagging along with me to sleepover camp. She was the last person I wanted hanging around. But what I didn't expect was that I'd be the one to get homesick and she'd be my biggest comfort.

Grown-up but not grown apart!
From left to right: me, Deed, Mandy

That's just one example of how important my sister was to me. When I was a girl, no one could get under my skin more than Mandy or my younger brother, Deed. Sharing everything from our personal space to our parents' attention was tricky business. But we shared special moments, too—lost teeth, snow days, a new puppy, accomplishments, and disappointments.

Getting along isn't easy. It takes patience and hard work. You have to *try*. I hope this book helps you get through the tough times and make the most of the good times. After all, no one knows you like a brother or sister. And like a hug when you're homesick, no relationship can feel quite so good.

Your friend at American Girl,

Brooks Phillips

Contents

All in the Family

Sib•ling 8

Quiz: How Well Do You Know
  Each Other? 10

A Closer Look.. 12

Leader of the Pack 14

In the Middle 16

Last But Not Least..................................... 18

Quiz: Smooth Sailing? 20

I Hate Being a Sister!

Top 10 Most Annoying Things
  Siblings Do... 24

Pest Control 26

Quiz: When Are YOU a Pest? 28

Sooo Embarrassed!.................................... 30

How Bad *Was* It?......................................32

It's Not Fair!..34

Fire Hazards 36

Firebugs...38

Fire Extinguishers...................................... 40

Save Our Sweater 42

Quiz: To Tell or Not to Tell 44

I'm Sorry 46

Super Sister Extras

Sibling Constitution
Fancy Frames
Handy Hangers

I Love Being a Sister!

The 9 Nicest Things About
    Having a Sibling 50
Someone to Play With.................................. 52
Team Up! 54
Little Things Mean a Lot 56
Room for Two 58
Blue Without You..60

All in the Family

Whether you're **identical** twins or as **different** as night and day, whether you live under the **same roof** or **far away**, you and your siblings have one thing in common: **parents.** And that makes you **teammates** for a lifetime.

Sib · ling (sĭb'lĭng)

According to the dictionary, a sibling is "a brother or sister, someone with whom you share at least one parent." But what does the word *really* mean?

Siblings by Birth

Children who have the same mother and father are related by birth. They may look like each other and act like each other, but that doesn't mean they're born knowing how to live with each other!

Half-Siblings

Half-siblings have one birth parent in common. For example, if your mom or dad had a baby with another person, you and that baby would be half-siblings. But that wouldn't make your relationship only half as important!

A Bond Beyond

No matter how you're related, you and your sibling are linked together by common experiences and a lifetime of memories. Just remember, while friends may come and go, siblings are forever.

Step-Siblings

Step-siblings are related by marriage. When two people who already have children get married, those children become step-siblings. Whether they live together or with different parents, their relationship can be as special—and as challenging—as any other.

Adopted Siblings

If a child is adopted into a family, that child and the other children in the family become siblings, no matter what ages or races they are. You don't need to be related by birth or marriage to be related by love.

How Well Do You Know Each Other?

Take this quiz with your sibling. On separate pieces of paper, answer the following questions. Then try to guess each other's answers.

1. My favorite candy bar is ___.

2. The best birthday I ever had was ___.

3. If I could get either a kitten or a puppy, I would definitely pick a ___.

4. The book I have read the most times is ___.

5. My favorite sport to play is ___. My favorite sport to watch is ___.

6. If I were making my favorite sandwich, I would put ___ on it. I would never put ___ on it!

7. If I had to take either a spelling test or a math test, I would rather take a ___ test.

8. At amusement parks, my favorite ride is the ___. But you'll never get me to go on the ___!

9. The famous person I'd most like to invite to dinner is ___.

10. Someday I would like to be famous for ___.

How Did You Do?

More Than Half Right
You know a lot about each other. And that can come in handy for solving problems and getting along. The more familiar you are with each other's likes and dislikes, the easier it is to understand each other's point of view.

Less Than Half Right
Were you surprised by your sibling's answers? No matter how long you've known someone, there's always more to learn. Take an interest in each other's lives and spend time together. The more you know, the less likely you'll be to have misunderstandings.

A Closer Look

You're neat as a pin, and your sister's a slob. How could you be so different? It may have something to do with being born first, last, or somewhere in between.

First in Line

If you're an oldest child, you may have these take-charge traits:

Reliable People can always count on you to get things done.

Organized You've got a place for everything!

A leader You're a born boss, someone who takes control.

A perfectionist You try your hardest to make everything the best it can possibly be.

Conscientious You pay attention and try to do the right thing.

Baby of the Family

If you're the youngest, these personality traits may describe you:

Charming Everyone's attracted to your winning personality.
The star You feel right at home in the spotlight.
Affectionate If someone's feeling blue, you're quick to give a hug.
Outgoing You're not the least bit shy. You love to talk to people.
Persuasive You're a pro at getting your way.

Middle Matters

Living in the middle, you're likely to have some of these qualities:

The peacemaker If there's a fight, you usually play referee.
Afraid of conflict You'll do anything to avoid trouble with others.
Easygoing You're good at being flexible and going with the flow.
Loyal You stick by your friends and family through thick and thin.
Friendly You get along with everyone, young and old.

Leader of the Pack

They're the first to be trusted and the first to get blamed. Oldest sisters agree that being firstborn means having extra privileges—and extra responsibilities.

I get into trouble for things my siblings do because I'm the oldest and should know better.
—Amanda

I don't have an older sister to talk to the way my sister talks to me.
—Brandy

I'm never bossed around, and I get to take charge.
—Kayla

I like that my parents trust me to take care of my baby brother.
—Amanda

I don't ever have to wear hand-me-downs.
—Shannon

You have to be the first to try everything, such as school and braces!
—Meredith

I like being the oldest, because I know my brothers and sisters look up to me.
—Brooke

It's hard always having to be a good example for my younger siblings when I'm not perfect either.
—Naomi

In the Middle

Most middle sisters think they have the best and worst of both worlds. Do you agree?

My brother gets lots of attention because he's the youngest. My sister gets lots of attention because she's the oldest. Sometimes I feel left out and not special.
—Nicole

Just like an Oreo cookie, the good stuff is always in the middle!
—Brianna

I have younger siblings to take care of and older siblings to boss me around!
—Mariette

I wouldn't want to be the first child because you have to go through everything first. And I wouldn't want to be the young-est because all of my siblings would leave the house before me, and that would be no fun!
—Mackenzie

I'm either too young to do things that my brother gets to do or too old to do things that my little sister gets to do!
—Gwyneth

I have an older sibling to look up to and a younger sibling who looks up to me.
—Holly

When we play a game, it doesn't matter if we go youngest first or oldest first. I always get to go second!
—Bridget

I have to be a good example for my little sisters, but I don't get any of the privileges my older brother does.
—Sara

Last But Not Least

Being the baby of the family is something you never outgrow, no matter how old you get. Here's how some girls feel about being the youngest.

My brothers get to stay up late and watch movies, but I have to go to bed.
—Preston

I learn what not to do from my older brother's mistakes.
—Rose

My sister gets new clothes, and I get hand-me-downs.
—Andi

I don't like being bossed around by my older siblings.
—Priscilla

Teachers think that you will be exactly the same kind of student as your older sibling. It's hard living up to my brother's reputation.
—Kate

I like being the youngest because my sister gives me advice about things I don't want to ask my mom about.
—Katie

My sisters help me do my hair and pick out cute outfits.
—Jean

My parents aren't as overprotective of me because they've already experienced everything with my brother.
—Julie

It's cool having an older sibling to watch out for you.
—Elizabeth

Smooth Sailing?

Does your sibling relationship cruise calmly or toss on troubled waters? Circle the answer that describes how you might react in each situation.

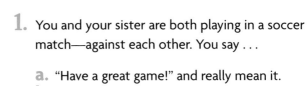

1. You and your sister are both playing in a soccer match—against each other. You say . . .

   a. "Have a great game!" and really mean it.
   b. "Good luck," but silently hope she messes up.
   c. nothing. And if her team wins, mutter "Cheaters, cheaters!" all the way home.

2. There's only one chocolate-chip cookie left. You and your brother both want it. You . . .

   a. split it down the middle.
   b. argue briefly until one of you gives in.
   c. get into a huge screaming fight that brings your dad running into the room, shouting "STOP IT!"

3. You and your sister both have friends over. You each want to play in the bedroom that you share. You . . .

 a. all play in the room together.
 b. trade off and avoid each other like the plague.
 c. both try to get there first and lock the other out.

4. On long car trips, you and your sibling spend the time . . .

 a. playing games such as Cat's Cradle.
 b. listening to headphones, finding your own ways to entertain yourselves.
 c. teasing each other and shouting things like "Quit touching me! Move over!"

5. When one of you gets a new haircut, no matter what it looks like, the other . . .

 a. says, "I like it!"
 b. doesn't really notice or care.
 c. makes fun of it nonstop for days.

How Well Do You Get Along?

Look at your answers to see what they say about your relationship.

If you circled mostly a's, your relationship is shipshape. You know how to get along, and you enjoy spending time together. Full speed ahead!

If you circled mostly b's, your relationship is staying afloat even though you and your crew aren't super close. Sometimes you make waves for each other, but usually you keep to yourselves.

If you circled mostly c's, you're in rough waters. Oceans of emotion are rocking the boat. It may take some work to keep this relationship from running aground.

I Hate Being a Sister!

From **brief battles** to all-out wars, sometimes it seems as if brothers and sisters were just born to **bicker!** Whether your sibling **teases** or **tattles**, breaks things or steals all the attention, here's how to handle sticky sibling situations.

Top 10
Most Annoying Things Siblings Do

What does your brother or sister do that drives you crazy? Here are the top 10 complaints from girls about their siblings' behavior.

10. Gets all the attention.

9. Blames me for everything and gets me into trouble even if I didn't do anything.

8. Breaks, ruins, or loses my stuff.

7. Punches or kicks me to get what he or she wants.

6. Follows me everywhere and wants to do everything that I do.

5. Bosses me around.

4. Takes my stuff without asking.

3. Teases me, calls me names, and says mean things about me.

2. Tattles on me.

1. Barges into my room without knocking. I have no privacy!

Sound familiar? Turn the page for tips on tackling these problems.

25

Pest Control

Do you know what to do when your brother or sister is bugging you? Be prepared for the next attack!

Bossy Bee

Are you bothered by a brother or sister who always tells you what to do? Instead of saying "Buzz off," try a little honey. Nicely remind your sibling that the best way to get you to do something is to ask politely, not to order you around.

Barge-In Beetle

Does your sibling bore through closed doors and invade your privacy? Make a sign that says "Please Knock." Give your sibling points for following the rule. Take away points when he or she barges in. Give your sibling a treat for earning a certain number of points.

Phone Fly

What's that buzzing sound on the line? It's your pesky brother trying to listen in! Chase him away by not giving him anything interesting to listen to. Save juicy details for when you know he's not around.

Closet Ants

To prevent them from marching off with your favorite clothes and toys, throw your siblings some crumbs. Set up a special box with things you don't mind sharing. Store your prized possessions out of reach.

Teasing Tarantula

The best way not to get caught in a teaser's web is to ignore the insults. It may not take the bite out of mean words, but after a while your sibling may grow bored and creep away.

Copy Caterpillar

If you do it, so does your sister. It's frustrating, but it just means she wants to be like you. Bring out the butterfly in her by helping her develop her own style. Compliment her when she chooses things on her own.

Tagalong Tick

How do you get rid of a clingy sibling? Explain that you need some time alone with your friends. Then offer to do something special later with your sibling. He or she just wants to be part of the fun.

When Are YOU a Pest?

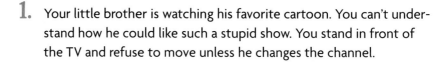

You might not realize it, but your own behavior may be bugging others. Circle the answer that tells how likely you are to act in each of the following ways.

1. Your little brother is watching his favorite cartoon. You can't understand how he could like such a stupid show. You stand in front of the TV and refuse to move unless he changes the channel.

   a. Yes, that's me.   **b.** I might do this.   **c.** No way!

2. Your sister is doing homework in the room you share. You want to listen to your new CD. She asks you to wait, but you put it on and start dancing around the room anyway. After all, it's your room, too!

   a. Yes, that's me.   **b.** I might do this.   **c.** No way!

3. Your brother has the softest baseball glove ever. You want to borrow it for a game, but you're afraid he'll say no. So you take it without asking. You're sure you can return it before he notices it's gone.

   a. Yes, that's me.   **b.** I might do this.   **c.** No way!

4. While looking in your sister's desk, you come across her secret diary! You've always wondered if she writes about you. You open the book and start reading.

   a. Yes, that's me.
   b. I might do this.
   c. No way!

5. You've been on the phone with your best friend for half an hour. Your older brother wants to make a call, but your friend's in the middle of an important story. So you ignore your brother and stay on the phone.

   a. Yes, that's me.
   b. I might do this.
   c. No way!

6. When your older sister has friends over, you follow them around and spy on them. That's what they get for not including you in the first place!

   a. Yes, that's me.
   b. I might do this.
   c. No way!

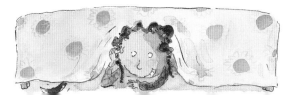

Pest Test

Give yourself two points for every **c** you circled. Give yourself one point for every **b**.

Bzzz! 9–12 Points

You're a super sister. You work hard to respect your sibling's feelings, privacy, and personal possessions.

BZZZ! 5–8 Points

You're learning to be considerate and fair, and that shows you care. But there's still room for improvement. Remember to think before you act.

BUZZZ!!! 0–4 Points

Pest alert! Your actions are more selfish than sisterly. The easiest way to change that is to treat people the way you like to be treated. Then they'll swarm around you instead of telling you to buzz off.

Sooo Embarrassed!

Has your sibling ever done something so embarrassing that you wished you weren't related? You're not alone! Here's a collection of humiliating moments.

My family was shopping, and my little sister was running around the toy department pressing buttons and making a lot of noise. We thought she was cute. But then she went over to the fire alarm and, thinking it was a radio, set it off! Our family had the reddest faces in the store.
—Allison

My family and I were at a Halloween party at my dance studio. My younger brother cannot dance at all. It was so embarrassing, because it was a dance studio! I tried to teach him, but it was hopeless. So I made him put on his Power Rangers mask so that no one would know he was my brother. He understood.
—Ashleigh

My brother was mad about having to go to my piano recital, so in the middle of my song, he started to sing along. I was so embarrassed, but I decided to act as if I had planned it. I had my brother come onstage to thank him, which embarrassed HIM!
—Karen

Once, at an ice cream parlor, my brother tried to feed ice cream to his make-believe friend Mugglewump. I wanted to curl up and die because everyone was staring at my brother dropping choc-olate ice cream into thin air!
—Lydia

I was opening a present at my birth-day party, and my brother said, "You already have one of those." I told him to be quiet, but he was right. My guest looked really embarrassed.
—Sarah

How Bad *Was* It?

Pretty Bad

My baby sister spit up all over my clothes at my third-grade open house. I knew making a scene would just draw more attention to me, so all I did was laugh!
—Alison

Not That Bad

My little sister sings at stores. Usually she's out of tune and doesn't know the words! But I just pretend she's doing a great job and ignore people's comments and looks. I think she's cute for being three.
—Victoria

The silly things your sibling does may make you uncomfortable, but they're probably not that noticeable to other people. In fact, if your sibling is little, people probably think whatever he or she does is cute.

Horror

Where does your most embarrassing moment fall on the Horror Meter? No matter how humiliating it felt, it probably wasn't as bad as you think.

When a sibling does something that makes you feel like the center of unwanted attention, try to grin and bear it—especially if it was an accident. If you don't make a big deal about it, chances are no one else will either.

Awful!

When my brother and I were shopping, he shouted, "Hey, why don't we get you a new bra? Do you like this one with Barney on it?" I got so red because this group of cool teenage girls started laughing at me.

—Emma

When your sibling's behavior is really out of control, try to remember that real friends don't judge you by your sibling's actions. When was the last time *you* dropped a friend because of something her brother or sister did?

It's Not Fair!

In the case of *You vs. Your Sibling*, sometimes you may feel as if there's no justice! But take a look at the facts. Can your case be settled like any of these?

I always get stuck babysitting for my little brother. My parents expect me to just drop whatever I'm doing to take care of him.

Judge's Ruling: It's nice that your parents can trust and depend on you. Let them know that you're glad to help out, but ask if you can work out a schedule that allows you to have some time to yourself, too.

My sister is smart, pretty, and good at everything from karate to ballet. Everyone thinks she's perfect. Next to her, I can't do anything right!

Judge's Ruling: It's not easy to follow in the footsteps of a star sibling. But instead of worrying about how to be more like her, step out of her shadow and develop your own style. If you focus on things you love to do, your talent will shine through.

My little sister is so spoiled! She has half the chores I do, and twice as many toys and clothes. She gets everything she wants.

Judge's Ruling: Does she really? Your sister may not think so. She gets bossed around. She gets teased. She gets left out of things because she's "too little." So try not to look down on her. She probably looks up to you.

Whenever a fight breaks out between my younger brother and me, I always get blamed. He never seems to get into trouble for anything.

Judge's Ruling: Your parents may expect more of you because you're older. But you shouldn't have to take the heat for things that aren't your fault. Find a quiet time to talk to your parents honestly and work on ways to solve the problem together.

My older sister has Down's syndrome, and everything revolves around her. Nobody cares about me or pays any attention to me.

Judge's Ruling: A sibling with special needs is bound to take away a lot of your parents' time and energy—but not their love. Ask if they can set aside some special time that's just for you. A little goes a long way.

Fire Hazards

Warning! Certain conditions can turn on the heat and cause tempers to flare. Learn to spot these situations so that you can proceed with caution.

Close Quarters

Living under one roof can lead to lots of friction. You bump into each other in the bathroom, crowd each other in the car, and trip over each other's stuff. Sometimes there's no way to avoid getting in each other's faces. But if you respect your sibling's space and personal belongings, he or she will probably do the same. Work together to figure out a bathroom schedule, a system for storing your stuff, and places to go for privacy.

Boredom

Sometimes fights break out when there's simply nothing better to do. Long trips, rainy days, waiting in line—any of these can send people's patience up in smoke. It's hard not to pinch, poke, and pester just to pass the time. So if you're feeling fidgety, entertain yourselves with games, songs, or jokes instead of taking your boredom out on each other.

Monster Moods

Steer clear of a steaming sibling. If your sister is stressed about a test, don't go running into her room while she's studying. If your brother's just been grounded, it's probably not a good time to ask if you can borrow his bike. Bad moods mean bad timing. And remember, when you're hot under the collar, don't take it out on your siblings.

May I borrow your bike?

Play It Safe

Remember these tips to help you keep your cool in a heated situation:

Stay calm. When you feel like you're about to boil over, take a deep breath. Count to ten or say the alphabet backward.

Use your head. Before saying or doing something you might regret, ask yourself: Is it worth getting into a huge fight, or will that only make the situation worse?

Find the nearest exit. Walk the dog, jump rope, or take a bath. If you're stuck where you are, such as in a car, try wearing headphones.

Firebugs

Not all fires can be prevented. But when sparks fly, don't fan the flames like these hotheads do.

Name-Caller

Says the meanest things she can think of. She doesn't care how badly her cruel words hurt her sibling's feelings.

Crybaby

Uses tears and tantrums to get what she wants. Her whining is wearing on the whole family's nerves.

Tattler

Runs for help instead of trying to work things out. She constantly interrupts her parents and breaks her sibling's trust.

Bully

Uses threats and physical force to push everyone around. No one stands a chance around her.

Fire Extinguishers

After a big blaze, the best way to put out the flames and prevent future flare-ups is with communication. Follow these tips for talking out problems.

2. Explain Why You're Angry

Describe how you feel instead of criticizing your sibling's actions. For example, say "When you come into my room without asking, it makes me feel as if I have no privacy" instead of "You always barge into my room! Why can't you ever knock?"

1. Cool Off

It's hard to listen when you've got steam coming out of your ears. Wait until the heat of the moment has passed before you try talking to each other. Otherwise you'll end up right back where you started.

3. Let Your Sibling Talk

Give your sibling a chance to explain how he or she feels. Don't interrupt, even if your sibling says something that makes you mad or that you think is untrue.

4. Try to Understand

If you're having trouble seeing your sibling's point of view, put yourself in his or her shoes. For example, how would you feel if your sister's door was always closed, keeping you out?

5. Agree to Disagree

Sometimes you can't see eye to eye no matter how hard you try. It's O.K. to have different opinions. You can still agree that you're sorry and that you're ready to move on.

6. Brainstorm Solutions

Work together to come up with ways to solve the problem. Can you agree on certain times when your door is open and others when your room is off-limits? You may have to compromise. That means each of you gives a little to meet in the middle.

Save Our Sweater

Sharing isn't always easy, but these basic bargaining tips can help you avoid snags and keep your sibling relationship from unraveling.

Take Turns

Agree to alternate. One of you gets the sweater on even-numbered days, the other on odd days. Or each of you gets it for a week at a time. Be sure to give it back on time and in the same condition as when you got it.

Swap

Are you willing to part with your favorite baseball cap in return for that sweater? If you each have something the other wants, offer to trade. It can be temporary or for keeps—just be sure you're both clear about which it is, so you don't end up in another battle over your belongings.

Make a Deal

Offer to do a chore or some other favor in return for the item you want. Your sister may be happy to hand over the sweater— if you wear it when you return her overdue books to the library!

Split It in Half

Obviously this solution doesn't make sense for clothes, but it works great for things like a two-stick popsicle or a piece of chalk. To be fair, have one person do the dividing and the other choose who gets which half.

43

To Tell or Not to Tell

Some squabbles can be solved without getting a parent involved. Others call for an adult's help. Do you know the difference? Circle what you'd do in each situation.

1. You're watching your favorite TV show when your sister grabs the remote and changes the channel. You . . .

   a. go find Mom or Dad to tell your side of the story.
   b. tell your sister she can pick the next two shows if you can watch this one. It's the only one you really care about seeing.

2. You know your brother is riding his bike without a helmet. You . . .

   a. promise not to tell if he does your chores for a month.
   b. tell your parents so that he doesn't get hurt.

3. You're in your room trying to do homework with a friend. Your sister, who shares the room, won't leave. You . . .

   a. get Mom off the phone to come get your sister.
   b. agree to let your sister have the room in an hour if she'll leave now.

4. Every day on the way to school, your older brother twists your arm and makes you give him some of your lunch money. You . . .

   a. keep giving it to him. He's too strong for you to fight.
   b. talk to your parents in private about what's going on.

5. Your little brother borrowed your markers, and now they're all dried up! You . . .

   a. call Dad at work to complain. They were brand-new markers!
   b. tell your brother he can't use your markers anymore and then put together a box of other supplies he can use.

6. Your sister calls you "Stupid" because you have a learning disability. You asked her to stop, but she won't. You . . .

   a. call her "Fatso" and tease her about her weight problem so that she knows how it feels.
   b. discuss the situation with your parents.

What's Your Tattle Total?

Give yourself a point for every b you circled.

4–6 Points You know when it's your responsibility to work out differences on your own, and when a situation is serious enough to ask an adult to step in.

0–3 Points You're tempted to tattle at the wrong times. Ask yourself: Is your sibling doing something dangerous? Is he or she hurting you or someone else? Does the problem keep happening over and over again? If so, plan a time to calmly discuss the problem with your parents.

I'm Sorry

Kind words and generous gestures let a sibling know you're truly sorry. Here are some creative ways girls have apologized to their brothers and sisters.

One time my brother and I got into an argument. I felt bad, so I sent him a code inside a paper airplane saying I was sorry. He sent it back saying he forgave me.
—Manda

My brother and I are always fighting. But we make up by playing soccer with each other. The loser has to make the winner their favorite food. Then we eat, tell jokes, and fight some more!
—Dorothy

After my sister and I had a fight, I baked her a cake and wrote "I'm sorry" in frosting. She gave me a big hug, thanked me, and said she was sorry too.
—Serenity

My older sister and I have a "forgiving contract" that says we each have ten minutes to think about what we've done and how to prevent it in the future. After ten minutes, we get together and talk about it, and then we forgive each other. It works every time!
—Nicole

Apology Basics

Any apology can be successful if you follow these simple steps.

Make the first move. It doesn't mean you're giving in. It means you care enough to work things out.

When you say it, mean it. Anyone can tell the difference between a sincere apology from the heart and a sarcastic "SOR-R-R-Y-Y!"

Don't forget to forgive. Accept your sibling's apology the way you want him or her to accept yours.

Wipe the slate clean. That means putting the fight in the past. Don't hold it against each other in future disagreements.

48

I Love Being a Sister!

Working hard to get along creates a **bond** that's super strong. And when the fights fade, the **fun times** take over. So **celebrate**—siblings are great!

The 9 Nicest Things About Having a Sibling

A helper, a playmate, a buddy when you're blue—a sibling can be many things to you. Here's how girls ranked what they liked best about having a brother or sister.

I love having five older sisters to talk to about my problems, help me with my homework, and show me new hairstyles.

I get cool hand-me-downs!

9. Helps me with things like homework and chores.

8. Gives me good advice when I have a problem.

7. Shares toys, clothes, or other belongings with me.

A lot of times my sister's gone through the same thing and gives me great pointers.

My brother is special because he encourages me and helps me with anything I try—especially soccer.

No matter what happens, I know that my brother loves me.

always looks out for me and makes sure I'm included in games at recess.

6. Sticks up for me when I'm being teased or bullied.

5. Teaches me new things, like how to do certain sports.

The best times are when my sister and I crack up over nothing!

4. Listens to my secrets, hopes, and fears.

3. Knows me better than anyone else does.

When I'm sad, my little brother makes me feel better by smothering me with hugs and kisses.

2. Cheers me up when I feel sad.

And the number 1 best thing about having a sibling is . . . .

Someone to Play With

The votes are in—on rainy days or any day, siblings make great playmates.

Silly Sibling Skits

Make up funny skits together about your family in different situations. For example, pretend you're on a family vacation—in space! Or imagine you've all traveled back in time to the Wild West. What's it like?

House Scavenger Hunt

Have each person make a list of five items that are somewhere in the house. Then swap lists and have a race to see who can find the items on his or her list first.

Sibling Slumber Party

Make invitations and hide them under your siblings' pillows. Set up a cozy sleeping space with everyone's favorite stuffed animals, blankets, and other snuggly items. For midnight munchies, serve your siblings' favorite snacks.

Who Knows

Write down ten "house trivia" questions, such as *How many stairs go to the basement?* or *How many doorknobs do we have?* Read each question and have everyone write down a guess. Then go check the answers together to see whose came closest.

Team Up!

You'll be amazed at what you can do when you combine talents and work together.

Cleaning Machine

Instead of fighting over who gets stuck with the biggest chore, agree to do each one together. Offer to help your brother shovel snow if he will help you clean the bathroom. Not only will you both finish faster, but you might also make a dirty job fun!

Family Business

If you like making bead jewelry and your sister is good with numbers, start a craft business together. You can design the jewelry and she can keep track of sales and profits. When you pool your talents, you'll see your profits soar.

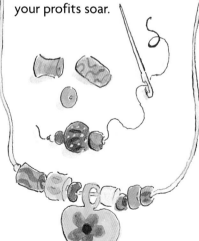

Group Gift

Give grandparents or other relatives a scrapbook of family memories. Divide the book into sections—one for each of you to decorate with photos, drawings, notes, and other personal mementos. Write a poem together about your family to put in the front of the book. Each of you can write your own verse.

Room Service

For anniversaries or other special occasions, treat your parents to a getaway vacation—right at home! Set up a room with lounge chairs, beach towels, and other decorations to give the room a tropical feel. Play your parents' favorite music, and take turns bringing them their favorite refreshments. Don't forget the tiny paper umbrellas!

Little Things **Mean a Lot**

A little kindness goes a long way!

"That's really good."
Praise your sister's art project or your brother's basketball dribbling. A simple compliment can make a sibling feel special.

"You can come too."
Include your brother or sister in your plans, if you can. It's always nice to be invited. And your sibling may be more willing to leave you alone the next time you really want your space.

"I can help."
Look for little ways to lend a helping hand. Is your brother late for school? Offer to make his lunch. Did your sister lose her calculator? Lend her yours.

"Let me show you how."
Take the time to teach your sister or brother something you know how to do, such as how to skate backward or how to blow a double bubble.

"Nice Try!"
Cheer your sibling on, whether she's trying out for the school play or goal-tending in the soccer championship. Your support is sure to bring a grin—and the courage to keep trying.

"Want some?"
Whether it's a bite of your sundae or a few sheets of your new stationery, a special treat is twice as nice when you share it—because both of you get to enjoy it!

Room for Two

Express Yourself

Choose your own pictures, calendars, and other personal mementos to hang on separate bulletin boards.

Reservations

Post a schedule that shows who gets to use the room when. Agree on play hours and quiet times. If one of you wants the room to herself for something special, she can reserve it ahead of time.

Personal Space

Make sure each of you has an area to call her own. Use furniture to divide the room, if possible. Each of you can set up your side any way you'd like. Agree to keep your stuff on your own side.

Even for sisters who are inseparable, sharing a room can be a challenge. Here's how to make the most of a *two*-tight situation.

Penny Jar

Pool your spare change and save up for something special that you both want for the room.

Twin Bins

For a cute way to control clutter, set up two large baskets, one for each of you. Whenever one of you finds something of the other's lying around, toss it in the basket so that she can put it away later.

Closet Divider

Is your closet so crowded, you can't tell where her clothes end and yours begin? Use wide ribbon to tie a big, bright bow in the center of the closet rod—then stick to your sides.

Blue Without You

Whether separated by summer camp or split up in different houses, being apart can make you appreciate each other even more. Try these tips to stay close.

Twin Times

Is there a TV show the two of you watch, a special bedtime routine you share, or something else you and your sibling normally do together? Keep up the tradition! Pick something you can both do at the exact same time every day or week. Imagine you're doing it together.

Photo Swap

Be a part of each other's celebrations and silly times. Take photos with a disposable camera and send the cameras to each other to develop. When you're missing your sibling, take a peek at the pictures—it's almost as good as being there.

MONDAY, JUNE 12

Look at the moon at exactly 9 p.m.

Pop-up Notes

Write a sweet or silly message on each sheet of a small pad of sticky notes. Ask your sibling to do the same. Each of you can post the notes around your room as little reminders of the other.

Funny Form Letters

If your sister or brother doesn't like to write letters, send a silly multiple-choice letter. Write a list of funny or serious questions with answers to choose from. All your sibling has to do is circle the answers and mail the form back to you. Include a stamped envelope for faster results!

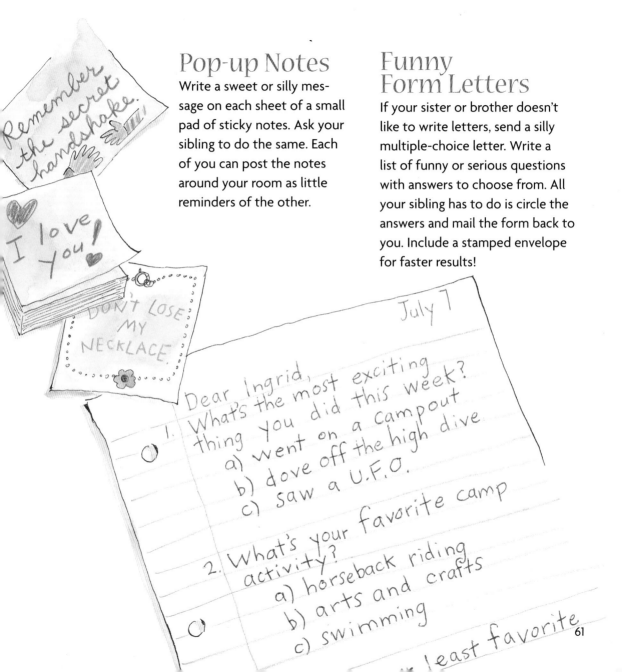

Remember the secret handshake.

I love you!

DON'T LOSE MY NECKLACE.

July 7

Dear Ingrid,
1. What's the most exciting thing you did this week?
   a) went on a campout
   b) dove off the high dive
   c) saw a U.F.O.

2. What's your favorite camp activity?
   a) horseback riding
   b) arts and crafts
   c) swimming

least favorite

Write to us!

Send your true sibling stories to:
Oh, Brother . . . Oh, Sister Editor
American Girl
8400 Fairway Place
Middleton, WI 53562

All comments and suggestions received by American Girl may be used without compensation or acknowledgment. Sorry—photos can't be returned.

Here are some other American Girl books you might like:

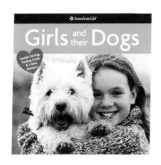

❑ I read it.

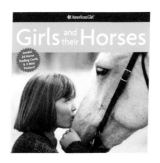

❑ I read it.

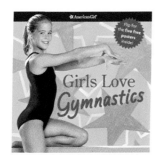

❑ I read it.

❑ I read it.

Super Sister Extras

Use the tear-outs on the following pages to brighten any room and to keep your siblings smiling.

Sibling Constitution

All siblings are created equal! Have each sibling sign and date this official vow to respect each other's rights. Tear it out and post it in plain sight.

Fancy Frames

Display favorite family photos inside these snappy borders. Punch out each frame, place it over a photo, and use a magnet or pushpin to stick it on your fridge or bulletin board.

Handy Hangers

These doorknob signs are sure to get your siblings' attention. Punch them out along the dotted lines and hang them with the message you want facing out.

Sibling Constitution

We, _____,
(your names)

in order to form a more perfect relationship and have a happier home,
do solemnly promise to do the following from this day forward:

- Take turns and share.
- Never borrow anything without asking first.
- Return borrowed items promptly, in the same condition they started in.
- Respect each other's privacy. No peeking in diaries, listening in on phone calls, or snooping through drawers.
- Always knock before entering.
- Give each other space when friends are over. No spying or tagging along.
- Try to talk out problems and solve disagreements.
- Listen to each other's side without interrupting.
- Take responsibility instead of blaming each other.
- Treat each other with kindness, respect, and forgiveness.

Signed: Dated:

_____   _____

_____   _____

_____   _____

Punch out here.

Punch out here.

Punch out here.